A Life Not Wasted

Michael Gunter

Gazelle
P R E S S

ISBN 1-58169-170-X
For Worldwide Distribution
Printed in the U.S.A.

Gazelle Press
P.O. Box 191540 • Mobile, AL 36619
800-367-8203

Table of Contents

Dedication

This book is dedicated to my parents,
Hal and Shirley Gunter.

Acknowledgments

When I fist began to ask the questions addressed in this book, I assumed that once I found the answers, I would be done with it. But God has been answering my questions now for over 15 years. In the course of these years, He has brought several key individuals, books, and passages of Scripture into my life, all of which have contributed to the application of His truth in my spiritual journey. I make mention of this only to give credit where credit is due. *A Life Not Wasted* is not the product of one man's spiritual quest. Rather, it is the collaborative effort of many people, divinely directed by God to set this man's life on the right course.

To those who have been directly involved in the production of this book, I would like to make special mention:

To those who have helped give form and order to my many moments of clarity: Keith Carroll and Kyle Wiltshire.

To those who have believed in this enough to contribute financially to this project: Harry & Barbara Bush, David & Kathy Godfrey, Hal & Shirley Gunter, and Heart of Love Ministries.

To my long time friend and brother in the journey, Danny Nicholson.

To my very best friend and confidant, my wife Tammi.

To these and many more, many of whom may never know of their contribution, I say, "Thank you." You are part of my journey.

Foreword

In his journals, Soren Kierkegarrd once stated that the introduction of a book should serve to "unclothe the spectators from their diverse preoccupations and get them ready for the real bath." I wholeheartedly agree with this idea as I begin to prepare the reader for the cleansing waters that lay ahead.

I first met Michael Gunter on the back porch of an old beach home in Charleston, South Carolina, in 1985. It was his freshman year of college, and I had been asked to share my thoughts on Christian ministry at a student retreat. As I remember, Michael and I enjoyed a lengthy conversation afterwards, discussing our desire to serve God through music. Not long after that first introduction, we began to write and sing songs together, and ten years later, after performing hundreds of concerts and reaching out to thousands of young people, we became the best of friends.

Everyone knows that friendship, like writing a book, is not a sudden thing. It happens over time. It happens after many late night talks in the back of a van. It happens after hours of prayer. It happens when you lean on someone everyday for a long, long time and their knees never buckle. It happens...and one thing is for sure, we should all thank God when it does...and I thank God for Michael's friendship.

As far as unclothing is concerned, it was C. S. Lewis who described friendship as "naked personalities." True friends are people who are unafraid to show what is inside, to share the pretty and the ugly, the dark and the light, to unveil their secret thoughts and dreams, to sacrifice their most precious gifts and talents—to give up their lives. The treasures of the soul are revealed in friendship.

I say all this about friendship because words come from

the soul. Words are the visible expression of an invisible world. Friendship has afforded me a "front row seat" to observe and experience the words of Michael Gunter. His expression is powerful because it is an authentic reflection of his faith and his life.

A Life Not Wasted is a book that reflects the soul and spirit of my godly friend. It is a labor of love and compassion that has been sitting in the harbor of his heart for years—waiting to sail...to reach the shores...to deliver a message of hope and love. I ask the reader to shed your clothing of "diverse preoccupations" and get ready for the waters of truth. These words will cleanse your mind, challenge your faith, warm your heart, and carry you towards a new place of being.

Danny Nicholson
South Carolina
October 2004

Introduction

Moments of Clarity

"What did you find, Dad?"
"Me? Illumination."
—*Indiana Jones and the Last Crusade*

Around 560 BC, a son was born to a wealthy family in India. Raised in the ancient Hindu tradition of his ancestors, he grew toward maturity and pursued a life of holiness. In spite of his strict adherence to the disciplines of the religious life, spiritual contentment alluded him. One day, while meditating under a tree, he purportedly received enlightenment concerning life, the dilemma of mankind, and the solution to this dilemma. He formulated his insights into what he called The Four Noble Truths and The Eightfold Path and began teaching them to a small band of followers. His name was Siddharta Gautama. Today, millions of faithful followers remember him as Buddha.

Buddha's quest for truth was motivated by two strong forces: A dissatisfaction with the prevailing system of belief of his day and a desire for spiritual fulfillment. These two forces led him to look beyond conventional ideas and seek a truth somehow missed by the masses. Buddha's enlightenment lead him to believe life was all suffering caused by unfulfilled desires; its only cure being the elimination of such desires. Today, even in a culture defined by indulgence and self-gratification, many have embraced the teachings of Buddha. In 1990, there were an estimated 401,000 Buddhists living in America.[1] That number grew to

1,104,000 in 2001—an increase of 170%. What began as a quest for truth by one man 2600 years ago has become a system of belief held by millions around the world.

History has had its share of prophets, sages, and mystics who have followed this same path, motivated by these same forces. Yet, in spite of this common search for truth, the conclusions have been various, and in most cases incompatible with one another. As a born-again believer in Jesus Christ, my biblical worldview has clashed numerous times with the views of those who follow other religions and systems of belief.

While a study of the various world religious and philosophies is quite fascinating and beneficial, what I am most interested in here is the moment of enlightenment. What did Siddharta Gautama experience under that tree in India? What did Mohammed experience in a cave outside the city of Mecca? What did Joseph Smith experience in the woods near his home in New York? What was it that so radically altered the course of these men's lives, compelling them to claim they had received the truth? (I have mentioned only three, but there have been many others with similar experiences.) And now, in some cases thousands of years after the enlightenment, millions of people embrace as their own the beliefs that came out of these three men's individual experiences.

Of course, we cannot know for certain whether these experiences were angelic or demonic visitations, drug-induced hallucinations, or the product of wishful thinking and fanciful imaginations. What we do know is that people do have these experiences, and that these experiences are "real" enough to convince them that they have been given the truth. And some of them have felt compelled to share this truth with as many people as possible. It is then up to those who listen to decide whether they believe it.

My own quest for truth has spanned three decades. While I do not believe I have come to the end of my journey, I sense I have come to a place that compels me to set in writing what I have discovered thus far. In this respect, I am not so different from those who have traveled this path before me.

In the interest of honesty to myself and the reader, I must clarify a few things:

The Origin of My Revelations

I do not claim to have been visited by an angel, nor have I ever heard an audible voice from heaven. I did not meditate under a tree or seclude myself in a cave. These revelations came to me in what I call "moments of clarity." I compare these moments to the lifting of a veil or the putting on of my glasses. It is when my understanding of God and the world around me suddenly comes into focus and I become keenly aware of things that have always been there but just beyond my mental reach. At times it has been a grand sweeping view of the landscape of reality, while at other times a little subtle nuance of a much larger picture. At first I could not maintain this clarity very long at all, maybe 30 seconds or a minute. And I never knew when it would come—sometimes while studying or praying or reading, sometimes completely out of the blue. It was only when I began to notice these moments and pay closer attention during them that I realized their importance. I began writing them down and revisited them from time to time, letting them take up residency in my mind. After awhile I began to anticipate them (though I still cannot conjure one up at will), and I learned how to sustain them for long periods of time. I now believe them to be of divine origin, little whispers from God. I have also come to believe everyone has such moments; but like me, either they fail to recognize them or are not yet able to articulate what they are.

I'm No Buddha

I said that I am not so different from those who have sought truth throughout the ages. I too am dissatisfied with much of my culture's present system of belief and I long for spiritual fulfillment. I too believe my moments of clarity to be revelations of the truth that has defined the course of my life, and I too feel compelled to share them with as many people as I can. But it is at this point that I break company with many who have gone on to establish new religious movements. My quest for truth has not lead me to abandon the old ways for something new. Rather, it has lead me back to the original truth—the truth that existed before men began to seek it. My allegiance rests in the God of Creation—Yahweh—and His Son Jesus Christ. The truth I have discovered is not original with me in any detail, but is firmly grounded in the Scriptures of the Old and New Testaments. I have no inclination to start a new religion or introducing a new philosophy.

My sole desire is to point people back to God, to worship and obey Him as He wants to be worshipped and obeyed. My theme in this life is "To know Truth, and make Truth known." This Truth is not some esoteric wisdom or secret knowledge, but a Person—Jesus Christ. For He Himself said, "I am the way, and the truth, and the life; no one comes to the Father but through Me" (John 14:6). Any deviation of these revelations from the truth of Scripture will nullify them and serve as proof that they are written in error. Should this be the case at any time, these insights should be dismissed as false.

A Simple Coincidence

Some may notice that the form of this book appears to imitate The Four Noble Truths and The Eightfold Path of Buddhism. I assure you this is purely coincidental. It was only after I had written the outline listing these Four Truths and the Eight Avoided Necessities that I saw the resemblance. In fact, I searched for a way to alter my pattern so as to avoid any similarity with the teachings of Buddhism. In the end, I decided to proceed with them as they were given to me and let readers assume the connection if they are so inclined. Rather than ignore the similarities, I have decided to point them out here so as to defuse speculations that feed on silence. Those who look for significance in such things are welcome to make something of this, but they will be disappointed to find these truths bear no resemblance to Buddha's Four Noble Truths, and the Eight Avoided Necessities are nothing at all like Buddha's Eightfold Path. My suggestion is to consider it one of life's humorous little ironies and leave it at that.

So with respect to you, my fellow seeker of truth, I offer this road map of sorts for the benefit of your own journey. May it guide you well.

Michael Gunter
January 2005

Chapter 1

The Avoidable Tragedy

"The contemplation of one's death
makes for a better life."

The Brevity of Life

In the summer of 1989, I attended two funerals. The first was for Janice, a girl I knew in high school. She lived 21 years before complications from Hodgkin's disease ended her life. As expected, the funeral was sad, as family and friends tried to make sense of a life cut so short. I attended the service with Sharon, another close friend from the same high school. We sat together and listened as the people who knew Janice remembered her brief life. They talked about her lively spirit, her valiant fight to live, and her love of shopping. We all forced a chuckle when someone suggested she was in heaven at that very moment, asking where the nearest mall could be found.

After the funeral, Sharon and I rode together to the gravesite. I remember the awkwardness of the moment. People lingered long after the service, unsure of what to do next. Perhaps it was the harsh realization that Janice was gone that made it so hard to leave. Maybe some saw her grave as their last connection with her, and leaving meant letting go. Maybe they were just not ready for something so final. As Sharon and I walked back to the car, I found myself wanting to look back at the grave just one more time. I suppose that is a natural human impulse when a loved one dies. We long to be with them just one more time.

The second funeral of that summer came just two months later. Sharon was returning to the University of Southern California to begin her senior year when she was involved in a single-car accident. The cause of the crash was never determined, but the police said she died instantly.

Fifteen years have passed since those fateful few months, and so much has happened since the summer of 1989. I still think of Sharon and Janice from time to time, and I wonder what their lives might have become. We who remain have gotten older, but we remember them as they were then—so young, so full of promise, so much life ahead of them.

———•◦•◦•———

I have shared this story for two reasons. First, nothing sets our minds upon life like death. Ironically, it is often at the end of one's life that the clearest vision of life is gained. When a person is at the threshold between this life and the next, suddenly all the trivialities that used to be so important become irrelevant. I have heard it said that no one, when they reach the end of their life, regrets not having spent more time at work or more time worrying about the things they could not control. Instead, the relationships with loved ones are the things that mean the most. Those who know the end is near have the luxury of getting their affairs in order. Confessions are made; forgiveness is offered and sought; permissions are granted. These have nothing to do with material things and everything to do with relationships—both with other humans and with God. I wonder how different our lives would be if earlier in life we could somehow acquire the clarity we gain at the end.

The second reason I have shared this story is because it illustrates a concept we all must face sooner or later: the tragedy of a wasted life. To be sure, the early deaths of Janice and Sharon seem tragic, at least for those of us who remain. We think of all the things these two young ladies have missed: love and romance, marriage, children, careers, travel, adventures, all the interesting events that have occurred in the world in the last fifteen years. Many people who do not have an eternal perspective would consider their deaths to be a tragic waste of life. But let us consider a few things before we make this assumption. Janice and Sharon both lived in one of the most beautiful locations in the world—on the shores of Lake Tahoe. They lived comfortable lives, never lacking for any of life's basic needs. They had loving families and many friends. Both of them had wonderful and unique experiences in their short 21 years on earth. What they lacked in quantity of life, they more than made up for in quality. The same cannot be said for most of the inhabitants of this planet. Those who suffer from extreme poverty, debilitating diseases, and crippling birth defects might very well prefer to trade 50 years of hardship for 21 years of relative ease.

I do not mean to diminish the loss of those who die so young, nor do I suggest that it is easy for the living to move on without them. As a parent of two young children, I imagine that I, too, would be devastated at the loss of either of them. Still, I think we are mistaken to consider a life cut short in this way to be a waste. There is something far worse than an early death—a long life that never became what it was meant to be.

Dr. Marx and the Meaning of Life

Dr. Marx was a professor of philosophy. When I met him in 1993, he was a frail, 80-something-year-old man who lived in the nursing home where I worked as a therapy aide. I only knew the man for two weeks, yet after all these years, I recall our one conversation as it if were yesterday.

"Dr. Marx," I said as I helped him into his bed, "what is your favorite thing to philosophize about?"

With labored breath, he answered, "That's easy—the meaning of life."

Intrigued, I could hardly wait for his final analysis. After all, here was a man who had pondered the age-old question for the better part of the twentieth century. Surely this seasoned traveler had some profound insights to impart to a novice still at the beginning of his own quest for truth. "What *is* the meaning of life?" I asked.

His expression was grim as he laid his head back on the pillow. "Nothing."

"Nothing?" I repeated, not sure if I had heard him correctly.

"That's right. There is no meaning to life." Dr. Marx went on to explain that he even doubted whether we really existed at all. For all we knew, he and I were simply thoughts or ideas in someone else's mind.

The more we talked, the more evident it became that this man, who had devoted his entire life to the search for truth and was now at the end of his quest, had come up empty-handed. His one remaining desire was to die and be done with the pain that tormented his frail body. Dr. Marx had no belief in heaven or hell, no concept of a spirit or even a consciousness that would survive the extinction of his biological shell. He was convinced that death meant only the cessation of life. This did not surprise me, for if life itself held no meaning for him, certainly death would be no different.

Dr. Marx—although he lived more than 80 years upon this earth—was the epitome of a wasted life. Some may think I am being critical of Dr. Marx. There must have been some redeeming quality to his life. He must have experienced love. He must have felt some gratification from having achieved success in his career. He must have gained some notoriety from books he had written or lectures he had given. Perhaps he had a hobby that brought him pleasure, or maybe he traveled to some interesting places and met some fascinating people. Certainly his life could not have been a complete waste.

Let us follow this line of reasoning and see where it leads. I know for certain he had a wife. She was quite a bit younger than he and seemed to care very much for him. I will concede he probably experienced love. He had achieved a level of success in his career, and he did tell me about some of the books he had written that had earned him a fair amount of money. Again, I will concede that he probably experienced some degree of fulfillment and satisfaction from his life's work. We did not speak of his travels, but judging from other professors I have known, I would assume he had visited some interesting places in his lifetime.

Let's do the math: If a person's life is measured solely by experiences in love, vocational success, interesting hobbies, and the accumulation of wealth, Dr. Marx would have had an enviable life. I suppose the people who attended his funeral probably commented that he had lived a good, full life. But the man I saw lying in that bed did not look like someone who had lived a good, full life. He was a miserable man who was hoping for only one thing—death, which he felt would put an end to his suffering. His younger, happier days had no more meaning to him than if he had not lived them at all.

As I said, Dr. Marx lived a wasted life. Despite all of his successes, the one thing that gives value to a human life was missing in his. He had failed to have a relationship with the Author and Sustainer of life, and because of this, he could not avoid the avoidable tragedy of a life without purpose. Now I do not mean by this that simply knowing God will prevent this tragedy from occurring. Knowing Him will only make avoiding it possible. One must learn God's purpose and submit his or her life to that purpose. Only then can a person live an unwasted life.

Unfortunately, I am afraid that lives are wasted more times than not. I know people alive today who are no better off than those who have already passed on. They spend their lives in hot pursuit of something that they think will give their lives meaning, happiness, and satisfaction. They believe they will find it if they get into just the right job or career, and so they expend great amounts of time and energy climbing the ladder of success, trying to make a name for themselves. They hope to find it in human relationships, and so they pray for spouses, and then they pray for children. They look for it in various hobbies and interests, and so they read books, learn languages, play music and sports, and travel the world, searching for something that will satisfy.

But no matter how much they succeed in any of these pursuits, life takes its toll: Jobs are lost to someone more qualified or less expensive, more marketable, or less aged. Spouses die; divorces occur; kids grow up and move away. Hobbies become too expensive, too time-consuming, or too taxing on an aging body. And these are the results for the ambitious ones, the ones who believe that what they seek can be found just around the corner, in the next relationship, in the next job, or in the next thrill. There are many, many others who experience this same emptiness, but lack the drive to do anything about it. These people simply exist, moving from one day to the next without direction or purpose. Their approach to life is purely utilitarian: They only do what is necessary to get them through to the next day. Many of them do not even recognize the avoidable tragedy of their situation. They assume that their experience is all there is to life. They simply do not know any better.

How have so many people become so lost? How could the truth of life have eluded them? Can anything be done to get them back on track so that they can avoid the regret of a wasted life?

I am very interested in such questions because, like you, every day I grow closer to the end of my life—to that moment when I will look back on the life I have received from God and determine whether I lived it as He intended, or whether I wasted it in pursuit of something else.

In the following chapters, I will explore four truths that I believe are central to our avoidance of a wasted life. Each truth answers a different question that has occupied the minds of humans for millennia. I am not suggesting that these answers will close the book on our curiosity about such things, for there is much to be gained in pondering the big questions of life. But I do believe they will present a perception of this life that is more in keeping with God's design for His creation. It is my sincere hope that these truths will be fuel for further inquiry and discussion, and in the end bring us all to a place of greater peace and assurance that we are living as God intended us to live.

Chapter 2

The Ultimate Question

"We can say that the purpose of God is that there shall come a time when He has a vessel in which and through which His glory shines forth to the universe."—*T. Austin Sparks*

Allow Me to Introduce Myself

Critics of early aviation used to argue, "If God had intended humans to fly, He would have given them wings." A modern critic of commercial air travel might argue, "If God had intended humans to spend six hours in a crowded tube at 35,000 feet above sea level, He would have given them shorter legs and larger bladders."

In spite of all its annoyances, traveling by air is a fascinating study in human interaction. It brings together people from all walks of life and forces them to interact with one another. On one particular flight, I met a tattooed and metal-spiked mountain of a man, clad in denim and leather, toting a metal case. At first, I was intimidated by what I assumed was a member of the Hell's Angels. As he checked his ticket against the number of the empty seat beside me, I prayed it would not match. God heard my prayer and sat the man next to me anyway. I eyed the metal case with suspicion, wondering what it contained (an Uzi?) and how he could have possibly gotten it passed security. Despite my hasty judgment, I soon learned that he was a body artist and the metal case contained the tools of his trade. He turned out to be a very interesting guy with an upbeat personality, and the flight turned out to be quite enjoyable.

On another flight, I encountered a mysterious young woman dressed in black. Her pale skin and straight raven hair reminded me of Morticia Adams. She stared at me through eyes darkened with black eyeliner as I approached the seat next to her. It was not until after I stowed my bag that I noticed her gaudy Victorian earrings and the occult symbol dangling from a leather cord around her neck. I don't know who was more uncomfortable—the gothic mistress of the night or this conservatively dressed student on break from a Baptist college. Conversation was somewhat slower with this young woman than it had been with Spike, but somewhere over the Midwest, we found ourselves engaged in a most interesting conversation about religion and philosophy. In spite of her dark appearance, she proved to be an intelligent woman with a rather pleasant disposition. Once more, I had an enjoyable flight.

Not all of my in-flight encounters have been quite as interesting as those with Spike and Morticia. More often, I sit next to people who are on business trips or holiday vacations. Our conversations rarely move beyond the typical obligatory exchange of flight destination and a few biographical details. "I work at a church," I tell the stranger with whom I share a two-inch-wide armrest. I tell him I am married and have two kids, and maybe that I like books and music, but not much more. It seems to me that we naturally fall back on that which is most easily explained in the fewest words.

While these things are accurate details of my life and will satisfy 99 percent of those who ask, they really do not describe the real me. They do not account for my quest for truth or the progress of my spiritual journey. Granted, most of my seatmates probably do not care to hear my philosophy of life. In fact, most of the people we meet throughout our lives do not care about our jobs, families, or interests; and they will most likely forget these details shortly after (or during) whatever conversation we might have. In most situations, the sharing of such biographical information is a social norm we all follow, especially as a courtesy to strangers we are forced to acknowledge on crowded airplanes, at business parties, or in any other situation requiring social interaction.

I am not suggesting we start bombarding strangers with revelations from our most recent moment of clarity. (Hopefully you have a friend with whom you can explore the depths of your spiritual inquiry.) I do, however, think we should be careful not to settle for biographical information as the sum total of our lives. While there is certainly nothing shallow or insignificant about our careers, families, and interests, the reality is that not much of what we do now will last throughout our entire lives. As I pointed out in Chapter 1, careers eventually end, children grow up and live their own lives, spouses die, and interests change. If we look for meaning in these things alone, or think that these things define who we are, then who will we become when life changes? If the purpose of a man is found solely in a successful career, what does that say about the guy who flips hamburgers or carries your groceries to your car? Is his life any less meaningful than the life of the president of some large corporation? If meaning is found solely in a relationship with another person, what does that say about those who are single, divorced, widowed, or childless? Are their lives less meaningful than the lives of those who have a spouse and two children? If identity is found solely in an exciting hobby or interest, what does that say about those who do not have the time, money, or ability to pursue such adventures? Are their lives less meaningful than the lives of those who do?

There must be something beyond career, family, and interests that will give our lives meaning and purpose for the long haul. There must be something that will carry us through this life, something that will remain constant in the face of change, something that will weather the storms of adversity. There must be something that will continue on into our retirement years, outlive our spouses, and stay with us when our children have moved away. There must be something that will continue to define our lives when we can no longer play sports or carry a tune. There must be something that transcends all these temporal human-centered pursuits, something that can define the core of our being without the possibility of diminishing with old age. This "something" is essential to who we are, and unless we find out what it is, we will be prime candidates for the Wasted Lives Club.

The First Question

And so we ask our first question: "Why are we here?" I believe this is also the ultimate question. It is the genesis of our spiritual journey. In seeking the reason for our being, we reach back to the very beginning to learn the purpose of the Creator Himself. Even those who do not believe in a divine Creator must seek the answer to this question by considering the origins of humanity. Sadly, without an acknowledgment of a Creator, the question leads to a dead end. Without a purpose in our creation, there can be no reason for our being. The answer to this ultimate question also forms the foundation from which we will answer all subsequent questions. We must first know why we are here before we can begin to understand where we are going and how we should get there. The answer to this question is the key that unlocks the mysteries of the universe and defines the course of our lives. It is truly the most important question anyone could ever ask—and its answer, the most important truth anyone could ever discover.

Being and Doing

Before we answer this all-important question, I want to take a moment to challenge a human tendency. Have you ever noticed how one of the first questions that is asked whenever two people meet for the first time is, "What do you do?" It rolls off the tongue as easily as "How are you?" Now, there is nothing wrong with either of these questions—except perhaps the fact that those who ask them seldom care about the answers. These questions are usually asked more out of courtesy than out of any genuine interest or concern. They are not unlike the questions about biographical details I mentioned above.

The "What do you do?" question is interesting because it reveals an important judgment we make about our lives: We value *doing* more than *being*. In other words, what a person does is held in higher esteem than who a person is. Even within the Church, most Christians are much more interested in the parts of the Bible that describe Christian activity and behavior than they are interested in theology. And many a sermon has been judged solely on the basis of its practical application.

Of course, practical application is necessary. We would be out of balance without it. But the fact that we have gotten it backwards (placed the "doing" before the "being") has resulted in many Christians practicing what I call "Checklist Christianity." Let me illustrate: When the average Christian talks about the condition of his or her spiritual life, what they are referring to is their participation in prayer and Bible study, their church attendance, and maybe the number of people to whom they have witnessed recently. If these Christians are consistent in these activities, they feel as if they are growing. If not, they believe they are suffering from spiritual dryness. So it is that most Christians evaluate their Christianity by the number of "checks" on this "list" of spiritual activities.

I am not diminishing the importance of the spiritual disciplines. But when we believe the sum of our Christianity is the doing of Christian activities without a firm comprehension of what it means to be a Christian, we suffer. The disciplines become acts of duty and obligation, rather than acts of love and devotion. The common result of this attitude is inconsistency and a lack of intimacy with God, which, in turn, leads to guilt and even doubt. As important as prayer, Bible study, worship, and witnessing are, they do not make a person a Christian any more than good communication, sexual intimacy, commitment, and a shared home make two people a married couple. Unbelievers can perform the activities common to Christianity, and unmarried people can perform the activities common to marriage.

I think we have arrived at this unfortunate misunderstanding because of many well-intentioned Christians who are emphasizing the doing over the being. Let's face it: Doing is much easier to explain and demonstrate than being. And many Christians have supposed that the doing

13

will ultimately lead to the being. But the commonness of spiritual stagnation among Christians indicates that this is not the case. Activity has simply led to more activity and not to much substantial spiritual growth.

What we need is a reorientation of our thinking—a reorientation that puts the being first. We must begin to let Christian activities spring up from the well of our spiritual being. But in order to change our thinking in this way, we must first understand what our spiritual being actually is.

For many people, such terminology (i.e., spiritual being) seems ambiguous. Perhaps an analogy will help. I just made the observation that unmarried people can engage in the activities commonly associated with marriage. So, what is the difference between a married couple and two unmarried persons who are living together and doing all the things married people do? It has to be more than a piece of paper and a nice ceremony. The Bible describes it as a spiritual bond—two becoming one flesh.

A similar observation can be made for our spiritual being. Baptism and church membership do not make a person a Christian. Rather, a spiritual union between the individual and Jesus Christ produces salvation. This conversion is different from the spiritual union that occurs in marriage, in that we do not become "one flesh" with Jesus, but the imagery is close enough for the Bible to refer to us (the Church) as the Bride and to Jesus as the Bridegroom. Our union with Christ is also a spiritual union, but instead of being one flesh with Him, we are said to be "born again" and now "living in Christ." I admit that this is not any easier for our mortal minds to grasp than it is easy for us to understand how two people can become one flesh. As a consequence, our reluctance to process this mystery has resulted in many failed marriages—and many failing Christians.

Not only is this difficult to understand, this "being united with Christ" is even more difficult to bring into reality in our lives. It requires the surrender of our will, the abandonment of our own ambitions, the destruction of our fleshly desires—in a word, death. It is the ultimate struggle of Shakespeare's question: "To be or not to be." I think the apostle Paul summed it up best: "I have been crucified with Christ; and it is no longer I who live, but Christ lives in me; and the life which I now live in the flesh I live by faith in the Son of God, who loved me and gave Himself up for me" (Galatians 2:20).

So far, this has not been good news! What I am suggesting sounds like the end of almost everything we have known. In a sense, it truly is the end of us. But once we have arrived at this end, we find that this is where the miracle of Christianity begins. Out of death comes new life. The resurrection follows the cross. As we share in the sufferings and death of Jesus Christ, so also we share in His resurrection. And this is great news!

Vessels for God's Glory

So what is the answer to the ultimate question: "Why are we here?" I realize that this has been a long way to go to get to the answer, but it was necessary to expose the error in order to see the truth. As I mentioned above, discovering our purpose for living requires us to reach back and understand the purpose of the One who created us. Written throughout the pages of the Bible as well as the pages of history, the purpose of God is expressed in His glory (or divine attributes). From the beginning of Genesis all the way through the book of Revelation, God has been at work revealing His glory to His creation.

God wants us to know who He is. He did this through

various displays in the Old Testament, the foremost being in
the form of light. In the New Testament, He revealed Himself
most fully in the form of a Man—Jesus Christ. John wrote in
his account of the Gospel that the Word was God and the
Word became flesh. God became one of us and lived among
us. John also wrote that although "no one has seen God at
any time; the only begotten God who is in the bosom of the
Father, He [the Man, Jesus] has explained Him" (John 1:18).
Elsewhere, New Testament writers proclaimed that Jesus
was the full expression of God the Father. Jesus is the glory
of God revealed to mankind.

Since it is the ultimate purpose of God to reveal His
glory to His creation, it follows that the purpose of God's
creation is to participate in this, His ultimate purpose. And
this is the answer to our question: The purpose of all creation is (to use the quote by T. Austin Sparks found at the
beginning of this chapter) "to be vessels in which and
through which God's glory shines forth to the universe."
Being a vessel for God's glory requires us first of all to be in
an intimate love relationship with God, and secondly to
allow Him to transform our life and our character into the
likeness of Jesus. As these two inner requirements become
realities of our spiritual being, they will manifest themselves
in two related outward expressions: 1) Our love relationship
with God will motivate and empower us to share that love
with those who do not yet know Him, and 2) Our imitation
of Jesus will enable us to love other Christians and encourage them to become more like Jesus themselves. You
see, the inward realities must precede the outward expressions. The being must precede the doing.

Once this truth was revealed to me, it became so obvious that I began to see it in almost every passage of
Scripture I studied. Soon it began to define who I was as a

person, and it became the guiding principle of my spiritual journey. Now it has become the foundational truth upon which I must live the rest of my life. Vessels for God's glory—my hope and prayer is that this image of yourself as His vessel will help you to know who you are and why you are here.

And we, who with unveiled faces all reflect the Lord's glory, are being transformed into his likeness with ever-increasing glory, which comes from the Lord, who is the Spirit (2 Corinthians 3:18 NIV).

Chapter 3

The Greatest Mystery

"Somewhere, something incredible is
waiting to be known."
—*Carl Sagan*

Dinosaurs and Outer Space

When I was a kid, my two greatest interests were dinosaurs and outer space. The past and the future served as bookends for my penchant for all things mysterious. As I read books about Triceratops and Tyrannosaurus Rex, I imagined there might be unexplored places on the earth where such amazing creatures still lived. As I turned my gaze toward the heavens, I pondered the possibilities of life on other planets, and I was thoroughly convinced extraterrestrials had visited our little world.

I remember listening to my dad's eight-track recording of the communications between NASA and the Apollo missions. Although I understood none of the technical terminology, the sound of it made me feel as if I were right there with Neil Armstrong and Buzz Aldrin. Much of my early childhood was spent digging for dinosaur bones in the vacant lot beside our house and looking through my dad's binoculars at the night's sky in search of UFOs.

My impressionable imagination was fueled in those early years by such television shows and movies as *The Twilight Zone, Land of the Lost, Planet of the Apes,* and *Star Trek.* In my teenage years, it was *Star Wars* and Indiana Jones that took me beyond the world of the ordinary. Even today, I enjoy good science-fiction stories, especially those that deal with time travel. I guess that in many ways I am still that wide-eyed little boy looking for adventure in the world of the mysterious.

I am not alone in my fascination. Long before Orson Welles terrified Americans with his 1938 radio broadcast of *The War of the Worlds,* people have looked into the night sky and wondered what might be out there. Ancient civilizations employed astronomers and astrologers, who saw their gods in the stars—myths that some believe hint at real extraterrestrial astronauts who visited our planet long ago. Judging from the popularity of the mystery and science-fiction genres, fascination with the extraordinary is alive and well in many rationally minded modern people.

I think the attraction to the mysterious stems from a human need to find out what's next—to know what waits for us around the next corner. As I write this, two probes are searching for signs of life on Mars. There is great interest in finding evidence that we are not alone in the universe. Even if life on another planet turns out to be nothing more than a microbe, many will accept it as proof that there is someone else out there—someone we might one day get to know. As intriguing as it would be to answer one of humanity's greatest questions—Is there life in outer space?—the discovery of a microscopic bug on Mars would not really affect the lives of people on Earth to any great degree. In fact, most of the world's population would probably not even know about it, much less care. There is, however, another mystery so great that every man, woman, and child on this planet will eventually find themselves deeply affected and very much involved in it.

The Second Question

Having answered the ultimate question, "Why are we here?" it is appropriate to ask the next question, "Where are we going?" This is mankind's greatest mystery, and for many, it is also one of mankind's greatest fears. Will this world eventually come to an end? Will history have a final page? If so, what will it mean for humanity? Will it ultimately be as if we never existed at all? These are important questions to ponder, and so it is no small matter that we now turn our attention to this greatest mystery.

There are many theories as to how the world will end. Science offers several from a purely naturalistic point of view: 1) The universe will, in time, succumb to gravity and collapse in upon itself. What started with a Big Bang will end with a Big Crush. 2) The universe will keep expanding, and eventually our sun will either burn out or blow up. The earth itself will either freeze or be incinerated by our exploding sun. 3) An asteroid or comet will crash into the earth, turning our world into a lifeless wasteland. Life on earth will go the way of the dinosaurs. None of these scenarios offer much hope for the future of our planet.

Another perspective observes a cyclical view of reality. According to this perspective, life on earth, as we know it, is simply the latest in an endless cycle of life, death, and rebirth. Other worlds with other civilizations have existed before us, and many will rise and fall after we are gone. Interestingly, ancient Mayan mythology set forth that we are presently in the fifth of such cycles, which, according to the Mayan calendar, will end on December 21, 2012. This date has already found its way into some Hollywood productions. I predict its importance will become more prominent as we near the end of this decade. Like the naturalistic perpecitve, this view does not offer much hope for us.

A third worldview does offer hope, at least for some. Most of the world's religions have a view of the end times that includes some kind of reward for the faithful and a judgment for the wicked. There will come a time in the future when God will have His vengeance on this rebellious world before restoring it to its original condition. Those who have placed their faith in Him will live forever either in heaven or in some other paradise environment. Those who have not believed will either be annihilated or suffer some kind of eternal punishment. The particulars vary from one religious perspective to another.

Humans will continue to speculate about the future of this planet. Books and movies will continue to offer scenarios involving cataclysmic events, cycles of reincarnation, alien invasions, and human evolution. Even those who adhere to a Christian worldview will continue to offer charts and timelines illustrating such events of the end times as the rise of the Antichrist, the rapture of the church, the return of Jesus, and the final battle of Armageddon. Many will continue to be intrigued by it all, while many others will be frightened and confused. A few will claim to have it all figured out and lead many to an end similar to the mass suicides that occured with the People's Temple in Guiana, the Branch Davidians in Waco, and Heaven's Gate in San Diego.

After the Smoke Clears

Because it is impossible to know anything beyond what

the Bible has already made clear to us, and because our Lord has said, "It is not for [us] to know times or epochs which the Father has fixed by His own authority," I have become much more interested in what happens after the smoke clears and the dust settles. Please do not misunderstand me. I am not suggesting that those passages of Scripture that describe the end times are unimportant. As part of the Bible, they should be given our careful attention and prayerful consideration. However, the final state of our being has much more to do with us than it does with the events leading up to that state. Whereas debate over the details and timing of the rapture and the great tribulation will continue, it is here that we can proceed with confidence. The greatest mystery has indeed been revealed. Without theory or speculation, we can know for certain the final culmination of our history.

I came upon this revelation some years ago while studying Paul's letter to the church in Ephesus. In the first chapter he wrote: "And he made known to us the mystery of his will according to his good pleasure, which he purposed in Christ...." I had read this passage before, but this time something was different. Suddenly, as if a gate had opened, my childhood fascination with mystery came rushing back—a fascination that, in my adult years, had been subdued by my acceptance of certain realities: Dinosaurs are long extinct, time travel is impossible, and even if life does exist on another planet, the possibility of contact is astronomically remote. Once again, I felt the excitement of pondering a mystery, and the truth that it was a mystery from God's Word that He was pleased to reveal made it all the better. I knew it had to be the greatest mystery of all time.

With growing anticipation, I read further: "...to be put into effect when the times will have reached their fulfillment..." These words put the mystery into the category of "future things"—"when the times will have reached their fulfillment"—that means the end of time! This was very exciting to me because I knew I was about to be given a revelation concerning the conclusion of history, and not just the history found in books and lectures—everyone's history, my history. Reading the next phrase, I felt like Indiana Jones deciphering an ancient text to reveal the location of the Holy Grail—giddy as a schoolboy. The culmination of human history, I learned, is this: "...to bring all things in heaven and on earth together under one head, even Christ."

Almost immediately upon reading these words, I was led to another passage that declared the same truth. In Paul's letter to the church in Philippi, he wrote: "Therefore God exalted Him to the highest place and gave Him the name that is above every name, that at the name of Jesus every knee should bow, in heaven and on earth and under the earth, and every tongue confess that Jesus Christ is Lord, to the glory of God the Father" (Phil. 2:9-11). Not only did this passage confirm the truth that history was moving toward a predetermined moment when all things would be subject to the lordship of Jesus, it also linked it to the answer I had received for the greatest question. Because we exist for the purpose of proclaiming the glory of God in and through our lives, how fitting that the culmination of human history would be the world's final expression of that purpose: "to the glory of the Father"!

Implications of Christ's Lordship

Now I must admit, the implications of this revelation did not occur to me at first. I was still basking in the glow of my initial clarity. In time, as I continued to ponder the reality toward which I now knew we were all moving, the weight of it became staggering. The lordship of Christ was no longer an option—acceptable to those who embraced Him as Savior and irrelevant to those who did not. These two passages made it quite clear. There will be a time when absolutely everyone will acknowledge Jesus as Lord, and not only acknowledge Him as such, but be subjected to His lordship. Some will submit to Jesus as Lord out of their loving devotion to Him. It will be an honor for them to bow down and confess their allegiance to Him. However, I am afraid most will begrudgingly bend to this submission. Their acknowledgment of Christ as Lord will be painful as they recognize the truth they had for so long denied.

Naturally, I wanted to be included in that first group, but I could not deny that I, too, was an active participant in the human dilemma. I had the same addiction as everyone else. There resided within me an insatiable lust for power, an aversion to the lordship of anyone but myself. What I thought had been uprooted out of my spirit when I became a Christian had actually lain dormant while I rested in my newfound faith. Through years of practicing "comfortable Christianity," I had secretly begun to take back some of the control I thought I had given to God. Little areas of my life that no one else would have even noticed began to be reclaimed. A selfish pursuit here, an imposed limitation there, a perceived right, a certain prejudice, an attraction to notoriety—portions of reclaimed territory that were suddenly illuminated by God's divine light became points of conviction in which I had resisted the lordship of Christ.

Even as I write this, several years after recognizing this truth, I still discover pockets of resistance in my soul, and I realize that I still need to resubmit to my Lord. But this continued conviction has led to a fresh determination. The knowledge that all of humanity is unknowingly speeding toward full submission to the lordship of Jesus compels me to prepare for that culmination now. Imagine the shock that such a transformation will be if one goes into it unprepared! In an instant, we will all realize just how much of our lives were held back from God as we see them all suddenly brought under His divine control. I can hardly fathom the jolt this will be to those who will have never considered such a conclusion to lives spent in blatant self-promotion and indulgence.

There it is, the greatest mystery. Admittedly, it lacks the Hollywood pizzazz of a flaming asteroid attack or alien invasion. The true answer just would not make for a good movie, for it does not allow room for humanity to rise up and save itself from certain destruction. I suppose some people will ultimately be disappointed to learn that our efforts to become masters of our destiny will conclude in submission to Someone else. It could be disappointing, that is, until we recognize the One to whom we will submit. He is the Master of destiny, the supreme Lord of His own creation. This culmination is simply the restoration of God's creation to what He originally intended. It is a return back to the beginning, but with a greater appreciation for the One who created us.

Thinking of it in this light, such a conclusion makes perfect sense. Any other end to human history would be just that—the end and a waste of life. This end, however, will be a beautiful, new beginning.

Chapter 4

The Universal Deception

"All that is not eternal is eternally out of date."
—*C.S. Lewis*

"The Truth Is Out There"

On September 10, 1993, a little television show entitled *The X-Files* aired its pilot episode. For the next nine seasons, legions of fans tuned in on Sunday evenings to watch FBI agents Mulder and Scully investigate bizarre cases involving the paranormal. It was kind of like *The Twilight Zone* for the 1990s. The defining theme of the show was Mulder's relentless search for evidence he believed would expose a government plot to conceal the truth about an alien invasion. During the course of the series, *The X-Files* developed a cult-like following of fans, ranging from the mildly interested to those who believed the show contained elements of truth about real-life conspiracies.

For me, the genius of the show was the pairing of its two main characters. Agent Fox Mulder was a man on a mission to discover evidence that he believed connected his sister's mysterious disappearance with the government's knowledge and cooperation with invading aliens. His philosophy was expressed in a simple phrase displayed on a poster of a flying saucer that hung in his office: "I want to believe." His partner, Agent Dana Scully, was a trained medical doctor and forensic pathologist assigned by the FBI to debunk his work and keep tabs on his investigation. Her approach to each case was one of cool rationalism as she sought reasonable, scientific explanations for everything the pair encountered. In one poignant scene in the movie, *The X-Files: Fight the Future,* Mulder and Scully discussed their unlikely relationship, which had developed during the course of the series—a relationship between him, the true believer and her, the skeptic. Scully lamented that her rationalism must have at times hindered Mulder's crusade. He replied that it was she that kept him honest. Ironically, it is Agent Scully who is portrayed as having a spiritual dimension about her character. She wears a crucifix necklace and occasionally refers to the faith of her childhood as she wrestles with the many unexplainable phenomena. Mulder, on the other hand, does not appear to have any faith at all, aside from the steadfast belief in his own quest for the truth.

Whether you agree with the premise of *The X-Files* or not, Agents Scully and Mulder offer a fair representation of the kind of spirituality that has arisen from the conditions of present-day America. Ours is a society defined by unprecedented advancement in technology and exploration. Scientific explanations abound for virtually every problem and question ever faced by mankind. We are exploring facets of humanity, our world, and worlds beyond our own that were hardly considered just a few decades ago. With the advent of computers and the Internet, our children have instant access to information our parents could not have even imagined. In such a world, we have come to expect reasonable and verifiable explanations for everything. Even when the best that science can offer is only a guess, it is most often accepted as fact. For most, faith is no longer a requisite for understanding the world; and even among those who consider faith to be an important aspect of their lives, it is not viewed as a necessity.

In an attempt to make sense of this world, some people have followed the example of agent Scully. They speak of a faith in God, yet they continue to seek explanations of the world that can be quantified, rationalized, and filed in neat, easily accessible categories. Other people are more like Agent Mulder. Disillusioned by the corruption and inconsistencies of human institutions, these folks want to believe in the extraordinary, the fantastic. They seek explanations outside of the realm of conventional human thought. They want to believe in something pure and ideal, something more than what they feel society is pressuring them to accept without question. However, they are unwilling to place their faith in God because, like so many other things, He, too, is seen as the product of a man-made religious institution used to promote the agendas of selfish men. While these two characters might at first appear to be opposites, they are both victims of the same universal deception: the primacy of this life.

The Third Question

Having worked through my first two questions, I found myself confronted with a third: "Is this life all there is?" At first, I was tempted to dismiss it altogether, believing that this question could be answered with a simple "no." But it was the ease with which I thought I knew the answer that caused me to give the question further consideration. And it was my temptation to dismiss it that led me to suspect that there might be a deception at work in my thinking, for it is the best of deceptions that slip by without notice.

Most people affirm a belief in the afterlife, and those who share my own Christian perspective further define this belief as eternity in heaven. Yet my observation of the actions and attitudes of people, including myself, suggest that there is a very different supposition at work just beneath the surface—the universal deception that this life is really all there is. Most of us obviously do not suspect we have been deceived, and we may even deny it, but the fact remains that many, if not most, of our decisions, actions, expressed views, and attitudes reflect the practical assumption that this life is the sum of our existence.

Perhaps a few examples would be helpful in the consideration of this line of thought:

• A group of Christians pray that God will heal a 90-year-old saint in the final stages of cancer. Why ask God to prolong the life of those who are standing on the threshold of heaven, especially when they are prepared and eager to take that next step?

• Reaching the midpoint of life, I have experienced moments of melancholy over the fact that my younger years are behind me. Such moments are nothing more than an idealization of my youth. They cause me to forget that the best is yet to come.

• Another consequence of these middle years is a sudden awareness that time is rapidly passing, and I have fewer years to do the things I want to do before I die. I live as if there will be regret in heaven over the things left undone on earth.

• Then there is the simple disregard for the consequences of our words and actions. We live as if our time on earth has no bearing on our condition in eternity. Do we not believe the Bible's teaching that we (yes, we Christians) will be judged for our deeds and be asked to give an account for our lives?

• Finally, the priorities we set for ourselves indicate a stronger connection to this physical world than the spiritual. We spend so much time, money, and energy amassing insecure fortunes and building temporal kingdoms, and we neglect the things that matter the most.

Why do we speak and act and think in such shortsighted ways, ways that actually could be deemed foolish in the light of eternity? We have been deceived into thinking that this present existence is the sum of our living, and that nothing of any real substance exists beyond this temporal life. Now when I speak of focusing on eternity, I am not referring to pining for our future home in heaven. Fixing our thoughts on heaven alone only tempts us to hunker down and tough it out here until we receive our heavenly reward at the end of this life. I am more interested at this point in gaining an awareness of eternity in the here and now—an awareness of the spiritual while we yet reside in the physical. This is what Scully and Mulder failed to recognize. And it was this failure that kept Scully looking to science and Mulder looking for little green men.

A Satanic Tactic

I have called this problem the universal deception be-cause 1) it is a condition common to every one of us, and 2) it is a false view of realty that blinds us to the truth. This worldly view of life is an intentional tactic of an aggressive enemy, an enemy who is committed to our downfall. He accomplishes his purposes by distracting us from the reality of the spiritual realm of which the physical world is only a part.

It is an ancient tactic once used by the serpent in the Garden of Eden to deceive Adam and Eve into lusting after a worldly prize—the deception that self-gratification was a higher good and of higher value than obedience to God's commands. It was used against Esau to deceive him into giving up his birthright for the immediate satisfaction of his physical hunger. It was used against Israel to deceive them into wanting a human king like the kings of the pagan nations of the world. It has been used throughout history against mortals to deceive them into believing they were worthy of worship as gods—men like Nebuchadnezzar, Darius, the Egyptian Pharaohs, Greek generals, and Roman emperors. And it is still being used today to deceive us into believing this life is our one chance to get all we can before it is over. "Eat, drink, and be merry, for tomorrow we die" is an adage that has echoed throughout history. It is still heard today among so many people who live only to indulge themselves with little or no thought about the spiritual consequences of their actions.

The only Person who has successfully resisted this deception has been our Lord Jesus. Satan used this tactic to try to deceive Jesus into satisfying His physical hunger in the wilderness; to participate in an attention-grabbing spectacle in the temple; to gain the kingdoms of the world the fast way; and to avoid the painful humiliation of the cross. But with every deception of the devil, Jesus resisted with a clear statement of His commitment to the real world beyond the physical realm: "Man shall not live on bread alone, but on every word that proceeds out of the mouth of God" (Mt. 4:4). "Do not put the Lord your God to the test" (Luke

4:12). "You shall worship the Lord your God, and serve Him only" (Luke 4:8). "Yet, not My will but Yours be done" (Luke 22:42). These statements of Jesus reflect a constant awareness that this world is simply one part of a greater reality. C.S. Lewis aptly described this present earth as an enemy-occupied territory of the greater kingdom of God.

As I have meditated upon the earthly life of Jesus, it has become increasingly clear to me that we, too, must strive to attain this same mindset if we are to keep this world in its proper perspective. A sincere commitment to the attitude reflected in these statements of Christ will enable us to keep our minds open to the real world of the spirit and protect us from the universal deception of this physical world. Such a perspective of reality will render this tactic of the enemy ineffective.

Eternity Now

In order for us to begin to embrace Jesus' perspective on the world, we must gain a new understanding of time. The Greeks understood time in two very different ways, using two words to differentiate between them. *Chronos*, from which we get the word chronological, indicates linear or sequential time—the constant procession of time from one moment to the next. This is the time we most often think of as we move through the business of the day. *Kairos*, on the other hand, signifies the "opportune time." We all experience kairos in moments when time seems to stand still, or when we lose all track of time because the experience is especially deep and intense. It is during these moments that we step out of chronos and into kairos. Within these moments, we begin to understand what "now" really means, because we have experienced something that is beyond mere time. We have caught a glimpse of eternity.

David Steindl-Rost, a Benedictine monk, states that "Eternity is not a long, long time. Eternity is the opposite of time: It is no time. It is as Augustine said, 'The now that does not pass away.'"[2] I like to think of it as the Eternal Now.

It is this concept of time and eternity that I think Jesus had in mind when He defined eternal life in John 17:3. In His prayer to His Father, He said, "This is eternal life, that they may know You, the only true God, and Jesus Christ whom You have sent." Notice that in this prayer, there is no mention of time at all. Eternal life, according to Jesus, is a relationship with God. Our concept of eternal life (the living forever) is simply the necessary condition for us to remain in a relationship with the God who has no beginning and no end. For us to focus solely on life without end is to miss the entire reason of why Jesus came to earth in the first place. He did not come just so mortals might live forever. He came that mortals might enter into a continual love relationship with the God who lives forever. It is in this sense, as we find ourselves growing deeper in love with our Lord, that we can say we have eternal life now. It is not something we must wait to attain in the distant future. Living in this Eternal Now disengages the universal deception and awakens us to reality—a reality that is new to us, but that is as old as time itself.

This present life is but a hint of the real life to come. C.S. Lewis referred to it as "living in the Shadowlands." From time to time, God allows us a glimpse of the other side—a moment of clarity, if you will. These glimpses are not enough to make us want to abandon this world just yet, but they are enough to assure us there is indeed another world out there, which is actually more real than this one in which we currently live. It is only when we begin to recognize this truth that we are able to understand that time really is not fleeting, and eternity really is not an incomprehensibly long time. Our fears about the passage of time will begin to diminish, and we will start living each moment more fully, seeing them as precious gifts from God. Interestingly, it is only as we understand the world beyond that we can truly understand and appreciate the world through which we are now passing.

If these few short years on earth were the total of our existence, what would be the point of living at all? We would all be fools to deny ourselves of anything our flesh desires. But if there is a world beyond, a world more real than this one, we must be careful not to become too attached to our little planet. If eternity is real, why not ready ourselves by living in the Eternal Now?

Chapter 5

The Unexpected Life

"Inevitably...a search for Jesus turns out to be one's
own search."—*Philip Yancey*

A 21st-Century Jesus

Last year, my family and I visited a community of
artists and craftsmen. In one of the shops, I was intrigued by the numerous paintings of Jesus. He was
portrayed in a variety of situations—laughing, leaning
against the ropes of a boxing ring, performing a wedding.
Though the settings were varied, He was always depicted as
a strong, ruggedly handsome man in His early thirties. It
was obvious the artist was trying to portray Him as the kind
of man to whom people would be attracted. In every
painting, His kind eyes and warm, broad smile gave Him an
earthy quality not seen in more traditional images of Christ.
I appreciated the artist's successful communication of our
Lord's humanness and approachability. This was the kind of
Jesus that would appeal to just about everyone.

There was something else communicated in these
paintings, although it probably was not intentional. This

Jesus was very modern-looking—a man for the 21st-century. He had very long, wavy, light brown hair, and His beard and mustache were stylishly trimmed. He wore faded blue jeans and a white T-shirt, the sleeves of which were rolled up to reveal a tattoo just above a very large, well-defined bicep. His complexion was dark—not because of a Middle Eastern heritage, but because He was tanned from the sun. He almost had a "Southern California" look about him. This Jesus looked like someone you might see at a construction site or on a stage at a rock concert. As I said, it might not have been intentional, but these portrayals of a decidedly modern, American Jesus communicated something more than the approachability we all want in our Savior.

It became apparent to me as I made my way to the back of the shop. There I noticed a man dressed in a painter's apron talking to some customers. As I approached, I was struck by the familiarity of his face. At first I thought it was the same face I had seen in all of the paintings. He had the same kind eyes, the same broad smile, the same muscular physique, and the same long, wavy hair I had seen in the paintings. At first I thought the artist had fashioned his modern Jesus after himself. I later learned he had used a model. Still, the resemblance was uncanny. And this resemblance led me to an observation: Separated from the historical Jesus by 2,000 years, we create an image of Jesus based on our own contemporary experience. In our desire to have a Jesus with whom we can easily identify, we perceive Him as one of our own kind. Not surprisingly, Jesus comes off looking a lot like the person we see in the mirror each day. This tendency is nothing new or unique. I have seen pictures of Jesus depicted as an African tribesman, an elderly Japanese mystic, a Hawaiian surfer, a Hispanic cowboy, and an Australian riding a motorcycle.

If such mental reconstructions of Jesus were limited to His physical appearance, I suppose there would be no need for concern. After all, no one really knows what the man Jesus looked like. But our thoughts about Jesus do not usually end here. They go much deeper, and rightly so, to His character, His thoughts, His view of the world, His very nature. And in this respect, we treat Jesus the same way in which we treat everyone else—we make judgments based upon His appearance. Therefore, it stands to reason that if we perceive a Jesus who looks like an American, we will also perceive a Jesus who speaks, thinks, acts, and reasons like an American. But He will not seem to us to be just any American; He will be "my kind" of American. This is a serious matter, for any attempt to take Jesus out of the context of His historical setting, while it may make Him easier to identify with, will inevitably result in a distorted understanding of who He was (and is) and what He taught. Consequently, any cultural reinterpretation of Jesus will distort our understanding of who He intends us to be as His disciples.

The influence of these cultural perceptions of Jesus may explain some of the variant views of Christianity among those who supposedly read the same Bible. One person believes faith in Christ will result in material prosperity and good health, while another is led by faith in Christ to embrace a life of poverty and martyrdom. Are we dealing with two different Jesuses altogether, or with two different perceptions of the same Jesus? Similarly, one person's commitment to Jesus is evident in the way she lives her life, makes decisions, and treats other people, while another who claims to be a Christian behaves more like the world than Jesus ever did. Again, are we dealing with two different Jesuses (one who demands all and another who permits all), or with two different perceptions of the same Jesus?

I am not the only one to recognize this conundrum. I recently heard a news story about the changing image of Jesus. The reporter keenly observed that in our present world, now characterized by the constant threat of terrorism, Americans want a "tougher Jesus." The Jesus who plays with children and says, "Turn the other cheek," has given way to a Jesus who rallies the troops and goes after the bad guys. I even saw an Internet depiction of Jesus with the face of President Bush. That image alone supports my view that many (if not most) Americans have a perception of Jesus that is radically different from the Jesus spoken of in the Gospels.

It is evident to me that we are suffering greatly from this new, culturally manufactured Jesus. This impostor has not only kept us from knowing the real Jesus, but it has deceived us into believing that our ungodly pursuits and self-centered lifestyles are acceptable and honoring to God the Father. The only way to rid ourselves of this deception is to allow God's Word to expose it for what it is. An honest examination of the life of the real historical Jesus, as recorded in the Gospel accounts, is our only hope of rediscovering the One whose name we bear.

The Fourth Question

We have contemplated the ultimate question and learned that we are here for the purpose of proclaiming the glory of God. We have pondered the greatest mystery and discovered that the culmination of Earth's history will be the summing up of all things under the lordship of Jesus Christ. We have been awakened to the universal deception and recognized that this physical world is only a hint of another world more real than the one we are now experiencing. In light of these three great truths, we now ask the fourth and final question: "How shall we then live?"

As we discovered with the other questions, there is no shortage of opinions on the matter. Watch the news on any given day, and you will see how people are living. Listen as your friends and co-workers respond to the events happening around the world, and you will hear them describe the way in which they think people should live. Watch them deal with the issues and problems of day-to-day living, and you will see what they deem important, sacred, and worth living and dying for. What you will discover is that there are as many ideas about how we should live as there are people who are trying to figure it out. But is there one right way in which everyone should live? Is there a way that would allow for the great diversity of people in the world, yet still constitute the essence of the one ultimate way of living?

The vast majority of people look to religion for the answer to this question. They attend churches, mosques, synagogues, and temples. They study the Torah, the Koran, the Bible, and the Gita. They examine the lives of Moses, Buddha, Mohammed, and Jesus. Some wear bracelets marked with the letters WWJD; others shave their heads and wear saffron robes; and some don *kippots* and prayer shawls. Many immerse themselves in the religion of their heritage, while others explore the faith and practice of another. In all of these efforts, people are desperately seeking to give their lives definition—to establish a pattern for living.

In my own quest for the ultimate way of living, I have become convinced that the answer can be found only in the Person of Jesus Christ. While others may have offered good advice for living, Jesus alone claimed to be the only true way to the Father. It is in Jesus alone that we will find the essence of a life pleasing to the only true God. It is only in the imitation of Jesus that any human will ever find real peace, real satisfaction, and real joy.

The Unexpected Life of Jesus

In my book *Defined by Glory*, I explored this idea of living like Jesus as part of the fulfillment of God's purpose for humankind. In the chapter entitled "The Lifestyle of Jesus," I examined some of the aspects of His life that we need to incorporate into our own: His obedience to the will of His Father, His compassion for people, His sense of purpose, and His lifestyle of simplicity.

Not long after the completion of that book, I was challenged to re-examine the Gospels to see if the Jesus of the Bible actually matched my perception of Him. God met me in my investigation and shattered my cultural perceptions. His Spirit led me to aspects about Jesus Christ that I had previously overlooked or ignored. The result was an encounter with a Man very different from the Jesus I had imagined. This Jesus lived a life and called others to embrace a lifestyle completely foreign to the prevailing view of my own culture.

As a white, Anglo-Saxon, Protestant male, born into middle-class America in the latter half of the twentieth century, I have been indoctrinated into the worldview that is defined by my culture. I have accepted, without question, certain values and opinions that fit into the world of white, middle-class Americans. The history I learned in school and observed as depicted in the movies convinced me that America has always been on the side of the right. America had won my independence from the tyranny of British rule; it had secured my freedom from the evil empires of Germany and Japan, and at that time, I had no doubt that

America was protecting me from the enemy of the day, the Soviet Union. It was my patriotic pride that caused me to get up at 4:00 a.m. on a cold winter morning in 1980 to watch the United States Olympic hockey team defeat the favored Russians. It might have been only a game, but to me it was one more reason I was glad to be an American—one of the good guys.

While American patriotism influenced my view of the world as a whole, it was the American dream that shaped my view of life at home. I wholeheartedly embraced the idea that I could become anything I wanted—an astronaut, scientist, or even the president of the United States! All I had to do was get a good education, work hard, follow the rules, and apply myself. There was no reason I could not succeed. Of course, success was ultimately defined by large houses, fancy cars, and enough money to buy anything I wanted.

Interestingly, as I think back to my years in high school and college, my worldview was shaped by and became very much like the things I saw on television. For me, the world was white, good-looking, and capable of virtually anything. And I, a product of the television generation, saw myself as one of those who lived on the screen. I wanted a house and car just like those I saw on *Lifestyles of the Rich and Famous*. I wanted to live out the adventures of Indiana Jones. I wanted to have a career like the rock stars I saw on MTV. And I wanted a girlfriend who looked like the girls on Baywatch. I wanted to be James Bond and Bon Jovi all rolled into one—James Bond Jovi. As I entered my adult years, my pursuits became just slightly more realistic: I would have been satisfied to trade in my dream of rock stardom for a chance to meet Regis and hit it big on *Who Wants to Be a Millionaire?*

It never occurred to me that my worldview might not be

consistent with that of Jesus. I had accepted His teachings about being good and honest and faithful. I was fairly consistent in reading the Bible, praying, and attending church; and on occasion I even told others about Jesus. Yet there remained a gulf between many of my views and those of my Lord. Somehow I had interpreted Jesus and Christian discipleship in a way that allowed me to maintain my American patriotism and pursue the American dream. Instead of allowing Jesus to conform all of me to His likeness, I had unknowingly conformed many of His views to my own view of what the world should be.

I realize that some will accuse me of saying that patriotism and affluence are unchristian. They might even say that I am un-American. But rather than answering these accusations in a way that might be construed as backpedaling, I will ask the reader to consider a few simple questions before making a final judgment.

Is it unchristian to have or pursue wealth? The best way to answer this question is to let Jesus speak for Himself. In His Sermon on the Mount, Jesus said, "No one can serve two masters; for either he will hate the one and love the other, or he will be devoted to one and despise the other. You cannot serve God and wealth." Later, when asked by a rich landowner what he must do to obtain eternal life, Jesus told him to sell all he had, give to the poor, and then follow Him. When the man walked away, unable to let go of his wealth, Jesus told His disciples, "Truly I say to you, it is hard for a rich man to enter the kingdom of heaven." Jesus clearly saw wealth as a hindrance to living a life that is pleasing to God. Wealth came between the rich landowner and Jesus, and it poses the same threat to us, as well.

Until recently, I assumed these passages applied to only those who were wealthier than me—conveniently placing myself outside of their jurisdiction. I live in a nice, but modest, three-bedroom house, and I drive a 22-year-old Toyota pickup truck. I am comfortable, but certainly not rich according to American standards. And therein lies the catch. Jesus was not talking about American standards of wealth—He was talking about wealth in general! It was during my preparation for a discussion on this very topic that the Lord brought conviction to my heart. While studying recent reports on the distribution of wealth, I discovered that the median annual income in the United States is $42,400, and the poverty line for a family of four is $18,000 ($9,000 for a single person and $12,000 for a family of two). About 2.1 percent of Americans live at or below the poverty line.[3]

Most likely you are not surprised by these figures. But a comparison to world statistics reveals a disturbing reality. Globally, the median annual income is about $5,000. That is $4,000 less than the poverty line for a single person living in the United States. That means that the poorest citizens in the United States are considered to be living above the world's upper-middle income, and the those at the median income level in the United States are among the world's most wealthiest people. This still does not give an accurate picture of the disparity between the world's wealthy and poor. The global poverty line is defined as those living on $1 or $2 (U.S. currency) per day. Currently, 1.2 billion people exist on less than $1 per day, and another 2.8 billion exist on less than $2 per day.[4] To put this into perspective, over half of the world's population make their total existence on less than the amount of money it takes to keep my 1982 Toyota pickup on the road. These hard facts brought a very uncomfortable clarity to the words of Jesus. Suddenly, my occasional complaining about not having enough money became so trivial, and my fantasies about one day becoming "rich" lost all their appeal.

My reality is that I am very wealthy. For reasons beyond my understanding, God has allowed me to be born in the affluence of America rather than in the poverty of a third-world country. I accept this as an unmerited blessing from God. As His blessing, the wealth I enjoy is not my problem, nor is my having it a sin. The point at which I get into trouble is when I begin to lust after wealth, place my trust in it, and believe I am entitled to it. The Bible says, "For the *love* of money is a root of all sorts of evil, and some by longing for it have wandered away from the faith and pierced themselves with many griefs" (1 Timothy 6:10, italics added for emphasis). My prayer now is to know what God would have me do with such an abundance of wealth. There must be a greater purpose than the maintenance of a comfortable lifestyle for four individuals.

Is it unchristian to be patriotic? This question is somewhat more difficult to answer than the previous one. Jesus appeared to be so indifferent toward national loyalty that patriotism did not even make the list of topics He chose to speak about. Being a Jew, one would expect Jesus' patriotism to have sided with the Jewish nation of Israel. Yet it was for those Jews (the scribes and Pharisees) who most appealed to their national heritage as evidence of God's favor that He reserved His harshest criticism. To presume that Jesus preferred one nation over another is to have too narrow of an understanding of His mission. When we step back to gain a more comprehensive view of Jesus' ministry, we find that His loyalties sided not with one nation, but with the entire world. His love for all humankind makes national favoritism irrelevant.

So, is it wrong for a Christian to be patriotic? In the absence of clear biblical teaching, I am left with a judgment I believe to be consistent with the overall message of the Bible. I do not think it is wrong for Christians to genuinely enjoy the country of their earthly residence, to support their nation's leaders and military, and to cheer for their country's Olympic athletes. However, we must always remember that our real home is not represented by any flag or national anthem. The United States is not my permanent home. And when it is time for me to leave, I will not look back. Having said that, I do believe patriotism is unchristian when it becomes arrogant elitism. Unchecked nationalism is akin to racism in that it considers people of other nations to be inferior to one's own kind. The same may be said for blind allegiance to a particular political party, religious denomination, or athletic team. The truth is, Jesus is not a white, Southern Baptist Republican with season tickets to your favorite sporting events. And the sad reality is, that last sentence would probably offend some Christians.

For me personally, I am honored to be an American. I truly appreciate the men and women who have sacrificed so much to ensure my freedom, and I try to live a life that would honor their memory. I am proud to fly the American flag in front of my house, and I even get goose bumps when I sing the national anthem. However, in addition, God has opened my heart to the people of other nations. He has given me a new compassion for those who live under oppressive regimes, those who suffer in extreme poverty, and those who daily dodge bullets and wonder if the person next to them might have bombs strapped to his chest. My prayer now is to gain a sense of brotherhood that transcends national and ethnic boundaries to include all people.

These two questions are just two steps in our journey toward a fuller understanding of the unexpected life of Jesus, yet they are significant steps. They encourage us to proceed down the path leading to truth. By now you have become aware that this path is not easy. You may be wrestling even now with its implications regarding your own patriotism and your personal pursuit of wealth. I want to encourage you to take these matters to the Lord in prayer. Be honest with Him about your aspirations, addictions, and prejudices. Ask God to reshape your worldview and to give you the mind of Christ; and then be ready to embrace the extraordinary things that He will reveal to you.

In the next chapter, we will continue this journey by examining what I call the eight avoided necessities of life. These include certain conditions of the human experience that are almost universally thought of in negative terms, and, therefore, almost universally avoided. However, when these human conditions are examined in the context of the unexpected life of Jesus, they will be seen in a new light. It will become evident that those things that most of us tend to avoid are actually necessary for our spiritual growth. I am afraid that the road will not become any easier here either, but the prize for having traveled it will prove that the journey was well worth the effort.

Chapter 6

The Eight Avoided
Necessities of Life

"In trials and tribulations the perfection of humankind is hammered out."
— *Thomas à Kempis*

Buddha Revisited

We began this journey by thinking about enlightenment or moments of clarity. At the beginning of this book, I noted that some people have felt compelled to pass on the insights they have gained from these experiences to others. The result has been a multitude of belief systems ranging from variations of traditional religious thought all the way to unconventional philosophical constructs. Given the path down which my own quest has led me, I thought it fitting to revisit our old friend, Siddharta Gautama. Although the actual percentage of devout Buddhists in our society is rather small, almost all Americans unknowingly hold a view of life that is consistent with a fundamental aspect of Buddhist philosophy. For this reason, I thought it necessary to expose it to the light of the unexpected life of Jesus.

When Buddha organized the tenets of his enlightenment, he identified the first of four "noble truths" as, "All life is suffering." I would not go so far as to say that all of life entails suffering, but I must agree that much of life is characterized by suffering. Only those who have been extremely privileged and sheltered from the rest of the world would be able to take issue with this assessment. Buddha's second noble truth states that "All suffering is from desire or craving." Again, I can only agree that much of the suffering we experience comes from unfulfilled desire. One need not look far to see that some suffering, such as accidents and illnesses, really are not the result of unfulfilled desire. Of course, a devout Buddhist would take issue with me, pointing out that the suffering from an accident or illness comes from the fact that such things prevent us from achieving what we desire. I will not argue the point. Instead, I will invite the Buddhist reader to suffer through this chapter and count it as part of his or her lot in life.

The third and fourth noble truths are the tenets with which I have the most difficulty in the Buddhist belief system. The third truth states, "If there is no craving, there is no suffering." And the fourth follows, "If you follow the Eightfold Path, there is no craving and, hence, not suffering." The "eightfold path" is the Buddhist's guide for eliminating all desires, which, in turn, cause all suffering in life. Only those who have completed this path can receive enlightenment and become ready for Nirvana.[5]

While I agree to a point that Buddha got the condition of life on this planet right, I think his solution is terribly mistaken. The underlying belief of Buddhist philosophy is that suffering is negative, and therefore should be avoided.

Consequently, Buddha presented a plan to avoid—or elimi-nate—suffering. In this respect, most of us would make good Buddhists. We do not like to suffer, and we expend great amounts of effort and resources to avoid suffering in our lives. Jesus, on the other hand, viewed suffering altogether different. As we shall see, Jesus and the writers of the New Testament saw suffering as necessary for spiritual develop-ment. And not only suffering, but several other conditions as well.

A New Attitude About an Old Problem

Acts 5 reports a situation in which Peter and some of the apostles found themselves in trouble for preaching in the name of Jesus. After a brief stint in prison (from which they were miraculously released) and following an order to cease speaking in the name of Jesus, they were beaten and re-leased. This much of the story is known to anyone familiar with the accounts of the early church. What I find so amazing is not the fact that they kept preaching in defiance of the order, but the way in which they reacted to such vio-lent opposition. Verse 41 reads, "So they went on their way from the presence of the Council, rejoicing that they had been considered worthy to suffer shame for His name."

Honestly, how long has it been since you suffered shame for the sake of Jesus? Or, consider a more probing question: When was the last time you avoided shame that would have come your way because of your faith in Christ? And for those few of you who have actually experienced some sort of persecution because you are a Christian, how did you re-spond? Did you rejoice? Or did you complain about what you were going through?

What are we to make about this notion of rejoicing in the midst of suffering? If this were simply an isolated event that took place in the Bible, we might be able to dismiss it as a special situation with no real bearing on how we should react to suffering today. But it is not. As we shall see, this appears to be the consensus of the New Testament. The frequency of its occurrence throughout the Scriptures prohibits us from ignoring it, if we are to be serious scholars of God's Word, that is. The frequency of this sort of event allows us to consider it reasonable to expect that we should incorporate such an attitude into our own view of life's troubling conditions.

During my investigation into the unexpected life of Jesus, I encountered two recurring themes. When dealing with the difficulties experienced in this life, the Bible indicates that: 1) our response to such conditions should be one of joy (or rejoicing), and 2) these conditions have a curious byproduct—namely, our perfection. In light of this revelation, and because these things are allowed into our lives by God for our own spiritual good, it becomes apparent that we must change our attitude toward them when they do occur. Admittedly, the implications are shocking at first, but this only serves to reiterate our dependence upon the Holy Spirit. Embracing the unexpected life of Jesus as our own will cause us to think twice before we adversely react to one of these so-called "negative" conditions. We may even discover that we are forbidden to avoid them, as they are the very things we need. Certainly, we will find that our griping and complaining has no place in accepting that which is meant to perfect us.

Before we examine these conditions, I feel as if a word of caution is in order. We must be careful not to slip off the other side of this mountain. The Bible does not suggest that we go out looking for trouble in order to prove ourselves to be more "spiritual"—trouble is adept at finding its own way to us! Nor do the Scriptures permit us to help others move toward perfection by inflicting suffering on them our-selves—life offers enough suffering as it is. We must also be careful to never suspect that God receives some sadistic pleasure by watching us suffer. Any of these actions or atti-tudes would be a perversion of God's chosen methods of spiritual development. The various conditions of life, whether be they perceived as positive or negative, are all worked together by God to produce the greatest good for those who place their faith and trust in Him.

The Eight Avoided Necessities

When contemplating these eight conditions, I have no-ticed that they are not equally distributed to all people. Some experience more than others—for no apparent reason. Perhaps you know of people who seem to breeze through life with hardly a scratch, while others seem to get clobbered at every turn. I have no explanation for this, other than that God knows what is needed and what can be endured by every person on this planet. I choose not to follow the path of Job's friends who sought to explain the reasons for his great suffering. Instead, I will attempt to sug-gest ways in which each condition might lead to the devel-opment of our Christian character.

Temptations—I have never met a man, woman, or child who was not tempted by something, be it food, drink, sex, speed, or the simple pleasure of getting away with some-thing. Temptations are the trials that test our faithfulness and obedience to the will of God. While the Bible warns us not to enter into temptation, it does not instruct us to elimi-nate it altogether. Rather, we are to trust in God to provide for us a way of escape every time we are tempted so that we might be able to successfully endure the temptation. Every temptation resisted is another step forward in the process of sanctification, and to eliminate all temptation would deprive us of a necessary aspect of our spiritual growth. Because God did not remove the first temptation from the Garden of Eden, and because He led His own Son to be tempted in the wilderness, we would be foolish to expect to avoid them.

> *Consider it all joy, my brethren, when you encounter various trials* [temptations], *knowing that the testing of your faith produces endurance. And let endurance have its perfect result, so that you may be perfect and complete, lacking in nothing* (James 1:2-4).

Death—It is said there are two guarantees in life: death and taxes. Death is not the natural state of God's creation, but it has become the natural consequence of the sin that entered into God's creation because of man's disobedience. For many, death has become their greatest fear, for it marks the end of all we know and the passing into the great unknown. Yet for all of its dread, death is that necessary step we must take in order to enter into the next life—the life, as was noted in Chapter 4, that is more real than this one. The apostles understood this and did not hesitate to speak about their deaths with an anticipation that makes many of us uncomfortable. "For to me, to live is Christ and to die is gain" (Phil. 1:21), wrote the apostle Paul. He then confessed to being "hard-pressed from both directions, having the desire to depart and be with Christ," yet also having the desire to remain "in the flesh" for the sake of his friends. And in 2 Corinthians 5:8, he spoke of a longing to be "absent from the body and to be at home with the Lord." Even Jesus used death to illustrate our commitment to Him over our attachment to this world. He said, "And he who does not take his cross and follow after Me is not worthy of Me. He who has found his life will lose it, and he who has lost his life for My sake will find it" (Matthew 10:38-39). This should not be mistaken for an endorsement of suicide or reckless behavior. Rather, it is the most graphic portrayal of a total commitment to follow Christ through this life and on into the next.

Suffering—While it may be uncomfortable to accept that we must all face temptation and death, it is even more difficult to deal with the seemingly random nature of suffering. Why is a child hurt or killed, while the drunk driver walks away unharmed? Why does the young mother receive a diagnosis of cancer, while criminals grow old in prison? Why is one person born severely disabled, while another is born whole? Why does a tornado demolish one house and leave the next untouched? Such questions cannot be answered, though many have tried. And as varied as those persons' answers may be, so are our responses to suffering. Some people are drawn closer to God by tragedy—their faith is strengthened through experiencing that which they cannot endure on their own. Others, however, fall away from God, blaming Him and expressing anger that He did not step in and do something to alleviate their pain. While suffering remains one of the most often cited obstacles to faith in God, we must still accept that it is a necessary part of life on this planet. It does not confound God in any way. In fact, He chooses to use it to bring about good in our lives.

There is no better illustration of this than the passion of our Lord Jesus. Never before has so innocent of a person suffered so unjustly, yet His own words affirm that it was the divine will of the Father: "The cup which the Father has given Me, shall I not drink it?" Elsewhere, Scripture teaches: "For it was fitting for Him, for whom are all things, and through whom are all things...to perfect the author of their salvation through sufferings" (Heb. 2:10). If it were necessary for Jesus to complete His mission through the way of suffering, how much more do we, mere human beings, need to complete this process?

> *Beloved, do not be surprised at the fiery ordeal among you, which comes upon you for your testing, as though some strange thing were happening to you; but to the degree that you share the sufferings of Christ, keep on rejoicing, so that also at the revelation of His glory you may rejoice with exultation* (1 Pet. 4:12-13).

The next two conditions fall under the classification of "semi-random" events, because there appears to be some degree of consequence affiliated with them. They are not as random as a tornado, in that they are sometimes the result of poor choices or an unhealthy lifestyle. Still, there are some who experience these difficulties through no fault of their own.

Weakness—No one wants to be thought of as weak. Gyms are full of men and women who spend hours pursuing the ultimate physique—namely, muscular and powerful. And office buildings are full of men and women pursuing the ultimate image—namely, strong and powerful. Whether they incorporate the power lift or the power tie, the goal is the same—they do not want to seem weak because weakness does not sell. This does not appear to be the case in the kingdom of God. In fact, God uses weakness to instill within us a dependency upon Himself. The apostle Paul recorded God's response to his own prayer for deliverance from a physical weakness: "And He has said to me, 'My grace is sufficient for you, for power is perfected in weakness.' Most gladly, therefore, I will rather boast about my weaknesses, so that the power of Christ may dwell in me" (2 Cor. 12:9).

Poverty—This condition is not all too different from the condition of weakness, in that no one aspires to be poor. Aside from the ability to satisfy a lust for material possessions, wealth offers a respect among one's peers and a sense of self-sufficiency. I have often heard people say, "I am not asking to be a millionaire—I just want enough money to maintain a comfortable standard of living for my family." That may be a noble goal in the eyes of the world, but self-sufficiency does not square with God's idea of a noble life. It seems as if Jesus had quite the opposite view of wealth: "Blessed are you who are poor," He taught, "for yours is the kingdom of God.... But woe to you who are rich, for you are receiving your comfort in full" (Luke 6:20,24).

Jesus did not simply preach an ideal—He actually lived it. Paul described how Jesus put His words into practice:

For you know the grace of our Lord Jesus Christ, that though He was rich, yet for your sake He became poor, so that you through His poverty might become rich (2 Cor. 8:9).

If we are to follow the example of our Lord, we must re-examine our simultaneous pursuit of godliness and wealth.

The final three conditions are unique in that they are

not random; we really do possess the ability to avoid them. The first two can be avoided simply by keeping one's mouth shut; the last one by opening it.

Ridicule—The old saying goes, "Better to remain silent and be thought a fool than to open your mouth and remove all doubt." I find it interesting that people seem more apt to follow this adage when it comes to matters of religious conviction than they do on any other topic. It may be our culture's religious pluralism and the emphasis on religious tolerance that keeps us silent, or it may be the simple fact that we do not want to sound stupid. Let's face it, the Bible is offensive. Its truth rarely agrees with the opinions of the world. People will get upset when you start talking about Jesus being the only way to the Father. They did not like it when Jesus said it, and they will not like it when we say it, either. But God anticipated this and provided us with some words that should help us get over this aversion to being thought a fool: "Let no man deceive himself. If any man among you thinks that he is wise in this age, he must become foolish, so that he may become wise" (1 Cor. 3:18).

> For the word of the cross is foolishness to those who are perishing, but to us who are being saved it is the power of God.... For consider your calling, brethren, that there were not many wise according to the flesh, not many mighty, not many noble; but God has chosen the foolish things of the world to shame the wise...so that no man may boast before God (1 Cor. 1:18,26-28).

These passages do not give us a license to be obnoxious, nor do they give us permission to intentionally offend someone just to prove a point. If we are going to appear foolish, let it be for our commitment to the uncompromising truth of the Gospel, not for our attitude or behavior.

Persecution—Much of what I said about being thought a fool could also apply to persecution. Ridicule is a form of persecution, but persecution can actually involve much more. I have known people who have been denied job promotions, had engagements broken off, endured verbal and emotional abuse, and had property damaged because of their faith in Jesus. And that is just here in the United States! Throughout history, and even today, Christians are losing their very lives for the sake of the name of Jesus. We who have had it so easy often find it difficult to imagine real persecution. Nonetheless, persecution stands as a mark of true loyalty to Jesus. In fact, Jesus promised that those who follow Him would be persecuted. This often sounds frightening to us, but Jesus spoke of it as if it were a good thing:

> *Blessed are those who have been persecuted for the sake of righteousness, for theirs is the kingdom of heaven. Blessed are you when people insult you and persecute you, and falsely say all kinds of evil against you because of Me. Rejoice and be glad, for your reward in heaven is great; for in the same way they persecuted the prophets who were before you* (Mt. 5:10-12).

Obscurity—Historian Daniel Boorstin observed in his book, *Creators*, that human beings have an innate desire to be remembered. This, he said, has been the motivation behind all the great works of art and architecture throughout history. When faced with the realization of his own mortality, man strives to create something that will outlast him, something that will tell future generations, "I was here!" Most of us will never build a great monument, compose a symphony, or create a masterpiece, yet the desire to make a name for ourselves remains. I have had to confess that this has been the primary motivation for nearly all of my endeavors in life. Even this book may be, in part, the product of my desire to be recognized and remembered! However, I am continually humbled by the example of Jesus. His repudiation of the attention of men brings me back to His center and reminds me that this life is not about me. Consider our Lord's teaching on what it really means to be significant in His eyes: "But many who are first will be last, and the last, first" (Mark 10:31). "The one who is least among all of you, this is the one who is great" (Luke 9:48).

> *The kings of the Gentiles lord it over them; and those who have authority over them are called 'Benefactors.' But it is not this way with you, but the one who is the greatest among you must become like the youngest, and the leader like the servant* (Luke 22:25-26)

Perhaps John the Baptist summed it up best as he described the goal of his own life: "He must increase, but I must decrease" (John 3:30). Among all of the lessons I have yet to learn about humility and finding my place in the kingdom of God, obscurity may be the greatest teacher of all.

Maintaining Balance

There are two potentially dangerous reactions to these eight avoided necessities. First, there is the temptation to dismiss them as too extreme—it seems to be too much of a challenge to our natural impulses to eliminate temptation, put off death, avoid suffering, scorn weakness and poverty, protect ourselves from ridicule and persecution, and disregard obscurity. That is why I included so many Scripture passages on the various subjects! These are not the ideas of an eccentric ascetic, crazy from too much time spent alone in a cave. They are truths from the Word of God, demonstrated in the unexpected life of Jesus, and revealed to a person who has spent his entire life trying to avoid or eliminate them. It is extremely difficult to accept that these are the conditions God uses to develop our Christian character, yet we cannot deny the clear teaching of the Word of God.

The other temptation is to become overzealous and go after them as if they were badges of religious devotion. Such behavior would not only be misdirected, but it could prove to be extremely dangerous. We should never intentionally put ourselves in the line of temptation, tempt death, seek out suffering, deliberately become weak or impoverished, invite ridicule or persecution, or fade into useless oblivion. Instead, we must allow God to chart our course through life. And when He sees fit to allow any of these conditions into our lives, we should endure them with joyful hearts and allow God to use them to bring about His intended perfection.

Buddha's eightfold path tries to eliminate suffering by eliminating all human desire. This logically leads to escapism and a disdain for this life. But the Bible's treatment of the eight avoided necessities helps us to understand the value of such conditions by redirecting our desire away from self-preservation and onto Christ-centered devotion. This leads us to an enhanced life.

It should be a tremendous encouragement to us that

God is willing and able to meet us where we are. He became one of us and has experienced all the difficulties that we currently face. The path He has laid out for us will eventually lead to a place where the eight avoided necessities will no longer apply. But for now, as His followers, we find ourselves on a road He has already traveled. May we walk as He walked.

Summary of the Eight Avoided Necessities
And how they shape our Christian character:

Temptations are trials that test our faithfulness and obedience to the will of God.

Death illustrates our commitment to God over our attachment to this world.

Suffering provides us with the opportunity for us to identify with Christ.

Weakness instills within us a dependency upon God.

Poverty helps us to resist the sin of self-sufficiency.

Ridicule tests our convictions.

Persecution provides us with the opportunity to demonstrate our loyalty to Christ.

Obscurity helps us to overcome the sin of self-importance.

Chapter 7

A Life Well Lived

"And in the end, it's not the years in your life that
count. It's the life in your years."
—*Abraham Lincoln*

Travels Through Time

I have an affinity for things from the past (old cars, music
from the Big Band era, black-and-white movies, virtually anything you might find in an antique store), and I
am especially fond of old photographs. My interest in such
items goes much deeper than simple curiosity about days
gone by. For me, these relics are windows to the past. When
in their presence, I am often struck by a keen awareness of
the people whose lives were enriched by them. I think of the
original owner of an old automobile, a couple slow-dancing
to "I'll Be Seeing You," a young woman gazing into an antique mirror and beholding the youthful face in its reflection. At times, this awareness has actually induced a
sentimental ache for moments gone forever.

I recall an especially poignant experience I had while
visiting the home of an elderly couple. The wife was a pa-

tient at the rehabilitation clinic where I was working as a therapy aide. In her eighties, she was dealing with all the aches, pains, and inconveniences associated with old age. It was our job to gradually reintroduce her into her home environment to determine whether or not she could safely return at the conclusion of her therapy. As I watched this old woman, frail and bent, struggling to maneuver her walker around furniture and through doorways, I began to notice the personal effects of her home. Knickknacks on a shelf revealed a fondness for cats, children's artwork affixed to the refrigerator indicated grandchildren, and magazines on the kitchen table suggested that either she or her husband enjoyed gardening. I had seen such effects in hundreds of homes of patients just like her. I saw nothing extraordinary or thought-provoking—nothing, that is, until I entered the living room. There, prominently displayed above a large brick fireplace, hung a pair of wooden frames that held portraits of a man and woman, probably in their mid- to late-twenties, both wearing the uniforms of military officers. The man was dashing—he had the look you might expect to see in the old Hollywood's glamorized depiction of war. In addition, the woman was stunningly beautiful. Likewise, she could have been a movie starlet or graced the cover of a fashion magazine.

I studied the portraits for a long time, wondering what life had been like for these two people at that precise moment that had been captured by the camera. Were they married or engaged? Were the pictures taken during wartime? And if so, were the two of them about to be separated? What hopes and dreams had they shared? What fears and concerns had they discussed over supper that very evening? I wondered about their families and friends, their interests, their hobbies, the things they thought about as they considered their lives and the world around them. I imagined meeting them. Would we have had anything in common? Would we have become friends?

My curiosity finally getting the best of me, I inquired about them. The old woman told me that they were photographs that had been taken of her and her husband during World War II. My suspicions confirmed, I was struck by the disparity between two moments that were separated by the bulk of a lifetime—one had been captured and framed, the other was being lived out before my eyes. In the portraits, I saw two people who still had decades of life in front of them. They were young, attractive, and most likely caught up in the excitement of the times in which they lived. Yet in the flesh, I was seeing before me these same two people at the other end of their lives: no longer attractive and no longer enamored by the novelty of young adulthood. Feet that once danced the jitterbug now struggled to get out of bed each morning. Bodies that had enjoyed years of life and love together now endured constant pain and discomfort. And minds that had once pondered the mysteries of a promising future now most likely contemplated the dread-inducing thoughts of a life soon coming to an end.

I left the woman's home distracted by this new awareness of the rapid passage of time. In their younger years, these two elderly people had been very much like me. And in the not-too-distant future, I will become very much like them.

Since that day, I have had numerous encounters with people, objects, and photographs that have elicited these same emotions. Such thoughts haunted me. I approached them with dread, and yet at the same time I found myself strangely drawn to situations which brought them to the forefront of my mind. It was as if I were subconsciously seeking them out, perhaps in order to continue processing through them, or simply in order to discover some hidden meaning within them. In time, however, I began to understand what this moment of clarity held for me: namely, that I, too, was moving steadily through time. I was getting older. The days of my youth were behind me, and I was transitioning through the various stages of life. For awhile, this awareness caused bouts of melancholy, until eventually it occurred to me that I really had nothing to fear. Growing older is a necessary quality of life. It is unavoidable. And then, in the midst of my introspection, I realized that I had a choice to make. I could either cling tightly to the present and resist the onslaught of the future—a proposition that surely would prove to be futile—or I could accept this progression of time as an exciting adventure and allow the moments to wash over me like water in a stream. Choosing the latter, I have found freedom from the anxiety of aging. My graying hair and the increasing size of my pants have become occasions for lighthearted jesting rather than cause for alarm.

I am well aware that such ideas will not be readily embraced by a culture that idolizes youth and worships the thin and beautiful. Nonetheless, the fact remains that we are all getting older, and no amount of Botox or positive thinking is going to change that fact. The sooner we accept this, the better we will be able to adjust to the natural progression of time.

The Life Cycle of a Generation

I have been musing over these ideas and emotions for several years now, but it has only been in recent months that I have finally been able to grasp the important truth of it all. It occurred to me that each generation has its time on earth, consisting of three distinct phases. In phase one, each generation starts out as a product of the previous generation. As the child of the older generation, it has no other recourse but to submit to its parents' rules and expectations. In time, this generation will enter into adulthood (phase two) and inherit the torch of power and influence. For 20 or 30 years, this emergent generation will call the shots, taking its turn in shaping the society. In phase three, the now-aged generation must abdicate its "moment in the sun" to the next generation that follows. Eventually, the original generation will die out and will soon be forgotten. In the reality of human existence, we are all just three generations away from oblivion. Our children need us, our grandchildren know and enjoy us, but our great-grandchildren will hardly give us a thought at all.

We could think of this as nothing more than a depressing reminder of our mortality. In fact, wise King Solomon dealt with this very issue in Ecclesiastes:

> *Thus I hated all the fruit of my labor for which I had labored under the sun, for I must leave it to the man who will come after me. And who knows whether he will be a wise man or a fool? Yet he will have control over all the fruit of my labor for which I have labored by acting wisely under the sun. This too is vanity.* (Eccl. 2:18-19).

My own initial grappling with this idea leaned toward fatalism. What, I asked myself, really matters in life? What am I doing now that will be remembered even next year, let alone after I am gone? In the grand scheme of things, what does it matter that I have been here at all? After careful consideration, I realized that my life was of little, if any, significance to the world at large. In isolation, these can be dangerous thoughts, and yet I had to work through them to get to the other side.

Happily, I did make it to the other side of this mountainous issue, and this is what I have found: In spite of the fact that we are all just "vapor that appears for a little while and then vanishes away" (Jas. 4:14) as James put it, another fact is that we are still here. There must be a reason that we occupy this particular place at this particular time—there must be more than merely our shallow perception of our own immediate needs. While my existence may not matter much to my great-grandchildren, it matters a great deal to me, and it matters even more to my Creator. The world did not celebrate my arrival, nor will it mourn my departure; yet my God has ordained the length of my days and the borders of my habitation that I may know Him in whom I live and move and find my reason for being.

So where does all this lead? What is the good of our being here? I will let Solomon answer this question: "Now all has been heard; here is the conclusion of the matter: Fear God and keep His commandments, for this is the whole duty of man" (Eccl. 12:13). You may be thinking, "Could that really be it—fear and obedience? Why conclude with something so elementary? Isn't this what we have been taught from the first day of Sunday school?" Indeed, it is. But the great tragedy is that billions of people have wasted their lives in pursuit of something else—something that was never in their reach to begin with. They waste their lives searching for fame and fortune, unrealistic romance, and a host of other pursuits, when the only thing that will endure is to fear, or honor, God and obey what He tells them to do.

In the final analysis, I know that this is the destination of my own journey. And thus, it is where this book must end. Each of the truths we have explored can provide for us a road map for our spiritual journey. They are markers along the way, pointing to our appointed destination.

• Commit your life to being a vessel for God's glory.

• Strive to submit every aspect of your life to the lordship of Jesus Christ.

• Maintain a firm conviction that this life is only a prelude to a more real life to come.

• Endeavor to live the unexpected life exemplified by Jesus.

• Seek the benefits of life's avoided necessities.

Following this path will not guarantee that you will find financial success in a high-profile career, have a happily-ever-after marriage, experience the thrill of adventure, or see faraway places. Who can say what the Lord may add to your life? It will, however, lead you to peace in the midst of turmoil. It will provide you with happiness in the midst of sorrow. It will enable you to make sense of a world that many times seems to be spinning out of control. It will provide you with satisfaction and fulfillment in what others see only as endless days of monotony and boredom. It will ensure that your life will not be wasted.

Time for us will one day come to an end. We will leave this place and enter into a new and better country—one of heavenly grandeur. Wouldn't it be preferable to stand before your God in the confidence that yours was a life well-lived? A life not wasted—God's desire for us, our gift back to Him.

Endnotes

[1] www.adherents.com ©2002. Created April 1999. Last updated January 6, 2003.

[2] The Music of Silence (San Francisco, California: Harper Collins Publishers, 1995), p. 12.

[3] www.census.gov.

[4] www.infoplease.com

[5] George W. Braswell, Jr., *Understanding World Religions* (Nashville, Tennessee: Broadman & Holman Publishers, 1994), p. 53.

Speaker Engagement Information

For speaking engagements or other information, contact Michael Gunter at:

P.O. Box 5513
Cleveland TN 37320

E-mail: michael@ncbctn.com
Website: www.michaelgunter.org
